ROOMS

Ready and Not Ready to Die

Gillian McConnell

PublishAmerica
Baltimore

First printing

At the specific preference of the author, PublishAmerica allowed this work to remain exactly as the author intended, verbatim, without editorial input.

ISBN: 1-4241-0952-3
PUBLISHED BY PUBLISHAMERICA, LLLP
www.publishamerica.com
Baltimore

Printed in the United States of America

For my brother
Phil Heywood
with love.

ACKNOWLEDGMENTS

Special thanks to Elliot Richman for his suggestions—his many suggestions.

Thanks also to Alexis Levitin for additional insights.

I am grateful to my editor, Alice Kuipers.

Contents

Death is no more than passing from one room to another.

—Helen Keller

Death hath a thousand doors that let out life.

—Philip Messenger 1583-1640

Every week through the seasons
I walk up the hill to the gray stone hospice
to be with the people who are ready
and not ready to die.
They die before I get to know them.

Room 200—Empty

The floor, lucent
from a wash of disinfectant.

Bed raised high,
stripped down to its mattress.

Next to a small empty bureau,
a chair and a garbage pail
lined with plastic.

Pastel walls
and a peeling ceiling,
the room is
like the body
that left.

Room 201—Josée Arpin

Sitting up in bed,
Holst's *Planets*
playing softly,
gazing at a tree outside,
she tells me that for her
there's a suggestion
of something on the other side.

Not a promise but a suggestion,
budded with cherry blossom.

Room 202—Robert Bradford

Robert, age twenty, died this morning.

In the bathroom
I splash cold water on my face,
mascara stinging my eyes.

Tonight I go dancing.

Room 202—Maria Caron

Outline of sexy underwear,
an opaque uniform stretching tight
across wide hips above
mahogany legs rooted in Nikes,
Nurse Trina washes her pale veined patient.

The job, often done quickly,
is deliberately paced,
each touch contains extra seconds.

Room 203—David Decker

He demanded service with abusive words,
a perpetual furrow between caterpillar brows.

Numbers etched on his arm
this man escaped the Holocaust
to arrive in this final pit
amid potted plants of tulips and hyacinths.

Room 204—Thomas Drummond

In a bridal dress, an eighteen year old,
pregnant with the patient's child,
sits by his bed, clutching his hand
as if this could keep him forever.

The boy's mother pours ice chips
around the champagne
in a plastic tub by the window.

The girl's mother arranges white roses in glass vases.

The boy's father, on his way from the airport,
arrives too late.

Room 204—Paul Edson

His wife stayed by his side for three days,
then left for an hour to go home,
take a shower and change her clothes.

When his wife returned, Mr. Edson was dead,
as if he'd waited
to do this last thing to spite her.

Room 205—Samir Faraj

Mr. Faraj, granted asylum from Iraq,
hung on the edge for a week.
Everyone thought he wouldn't make it.

But Mr. Faraj would have to hang
on a lot longer because
his daughter was blown up
on "Route Irish"
on her way to the airport
and would never arrive
smelling of jasmine
from their garden.

Room 206—Irving Gelfand

This man, a Holocaust survivor,
discovered recently,
that the love of his life,
a girl he'd married in Warsaw,
is still alive
living in Calgary.

While I was quietly removing
a stray towel from the pillow,
he said:

"Leba?
I thought you were dead."

Meditation Room

A man sits alone
with the faint staccato
of a woodpecker.

His lover is dying
surrounded by
wife
and children.

Room 207—Suzanna Hammond

Sparrows squabble on the window ledge
outside Suzanna's room.

She's been here for several days now,
eyes closed, mouth open,
thin fingers spreading over a prayer book,
her nails matching the petals of a rose
in a vase on the windowsill.

I ease up and tie her blue cotton shift
to cover that scar
and a single sagging breast.

I untangle the brush that looted her scalp
and put it back on the bedside table
next to a jar of anti-wrinkle cream
and a picture of a young woman
in a two piece bathing suit,
squinting into the sun.

Room 208—Nicholas Isabel

Paralyzed in a wheelchair,
his dancer body fouled out by
a baseball player's disease,
he wears a band around his head
from which a tiny bat, the smallest
of magic wands, protrudes.

Slowly he pinch-hits a letter.
A mosaic metaphor
escapes his frigid motor tract,
and ink edged copper wings
flutter south
with the other monarchs.

Room 208—Francine Jones

This seventy-two year old anorexic
with a deep and thorny voice lashes out.

We learn to be patient:

She has neither friends, nor family,
except a daughter who no longer speaks to her.

Wrapped in plaid wool,
propped in a wheelchair on the porch,
stained fingers trembling to her lips,
she lights a cigarette as ants disappear in file
through a crack in the concrete near her feet.

Room 209—Gerald Kerr

Though Mr. Kerr is palliative,
I could die before him.

Earlier I fed him scrambled eggs in bed
and later found his teeth
grazing in Tupperware in the bathroom.

I pull on rubber gloves, brush the dentures
and remember that I have an appointment
in the morning to fix a tooth
cracked beyond repair.

Room 210—Juliet Lacoste

Under the wakeful eyes of her daughter,
the woman with mild dementia
and apple red nails
is clutching her squirming grandson.

She buries her face deep
into his chenille covered body,
breathing in roses,
then calms him
with the seven dwarfs
who come home
to find their chairs broken,
the porridgc eaten
and Snow White fast asleep
with the Big Bad Wolf.

The baby finally sleeps,
and so does the woman,
never to be awakened
by that handsome prince.

Sun Room

The day of Princess Di's funeral
on TV, the casket
surrounded by flowers.

In the hospital's sun room,
beds and wheelchairs
surrounded by flowers
are men and women
who should have died before her.

Aided by a walker,
a man, trembles slowly
towards an empty chair,
his smile masked in flowers.

Room 211—Jo Martel

I knock gently
and put my head round the door.

In that instant before retreat
I see the doctor,
a Rosetti Madonna,
wavy hair dissolving into light,
one hand on her patient;
the other, on the child kicking
inside her.

Room 211—Thomas McCall

With the requested banana a la mode
I knock and enter the room of a man
who loves to talk when he's not in pain.

Slurping dessert
he says
he often dreams that he returns
to the place where his grandmother lived,
where chimneys rose to the sky
and the corner gossip shop sold
loose tea, girly tabloids
and milk in pint bottles with flat cardboard tops
that covered inches of yellow cream.

Room 211—Eli Morton

With concrete face,
eyes shut and
barely a breath,
he lies still.

A nurse bends close and gently asks
if he would like to see
a minister
a priest
or a rabbi.

"All three," he whispers.
"And we can have a round of cards."

Room 211—Empty

When I was young,
people passed on,
or away,
in whispers,
like the echo of falling snow.

Emergency Room

Being amid people in pain
reminds me of the time
I sat in my own haze,
waiting for a doctor,
amid a group whose
faces were vacant,
bodies coiled,
mouths drooping
and eyes...well
people, with little in common
but their pain.

Operating Room

Aged twelve,
drowning in Demerol,
I'm being taken to the OR
for an operation.
Navigated on a stretcher
to a brightly lit room,
where masked figures float around,
cottoned in antiseptic green,
I close my eyes,
breathing in rubber smelling sleep
and a cartoon of dreams.

Hallway

Delivering lunch to the patients,
I remember my own hospital tray.
It held a plate of slippery white rubber
sunk in a pungent urea sauce.
Tripe, they called it.

Room 212—Mary Nadeau

Mary Nadeau had her voice box removed
and talked in clacking whispers.

When I spoke to her,
I also spoke in whispers,
and when the doctors left her bed,
they spoke in whispers too.

Room 212—Empty

Checking a newly made up room,
pulling the wrinkles out of tricot sheets,
reminds me of
a starched nurse peering down on me
in my starched bed.
I'm twelve.

Everything was starched in those days.

Room 212—Jean Nolan

This morning we discussed the gender
of a blind patient
with small breasts and a small penis.

I now read aloud
while a tree on the edge of spring
brushes against the window
rippling Braille reflections
over the bed cover.

Room 213—Sylvain Oritz

I answer the bell
to a patient standing
with urine
trickling down skeletal legs
from a robust penis.

A week ago
he put his life
in a recording for the grandchildren.

His past power and present frailty
take me to my uncle who died recently.

Uncle Henry,
a man who had led a large corporation,
began to call me by my mother's name.

The last time I visited, tears grooved his face,
he hiccupped, then nodded off to sleep again.

I took him in my arms and hugged his bones.

Now I take a towel
to dry the man in front of me
and reach for a woolen dressing gown
to warm his soggy bones.

Room 213—George Oswald

Louder than a
caw of crows,
those black eyes
before he died.

Room 213—Empty

Where rocky mountains
rise into low clouds
I climb into my tent
to that thud of increasing rain on canvas.
I pull off my boots and socks,
gently massaging my colder foot
that had so recently worn
a ballet slipper.

Easing into a sleeping bag with a book,
I bite into a bar of
Cadbury's Fruit and Nut
slowly melting chocolate
in my mouth.

I stand in Room 213,
look out at Montreal drizzle
and go back to that place
where there is no death

Room 214—Samuel Page

Drunk on chemical cocktails
shot through the arm,
hooked up semi-conscious
with Fox News babbling
in the background,
an IV attached to his arm,
a catheter attached to his dick,
throat piped with oxygen,
he talked through swollen eyes
because his dried out mouth
contained only the remnants
of a tongue.

A stench surrounds the bed.
I leave to alert the nurse and fetch fresh linen.
He is leaving with nothing.
If this is dying with dignity, dignity is shit.

Room 215—Martin Quinlan

He said that he was happy
because
he would never
have to
shovel snow again.

Room 216—Sheva Rubin

Offering pastoral care,
Sister Amelie visited the patients,
spending many hours in Room 216
consoling Mrs. Rubin's husband.

Once plainly dressed and without
makeup, each week the nun changed,
beginning with a bounce in her walk,
colour in her cheeks,
followed by a hair cut and perm.

Eight months later, she divorced Christ
and married another Jew.

Room 216—Anna Rutter

Mrs. Rutter's face was shining.
A young man sat holding her hand.

I told him
his mother looked wonderful.

He told me
she was his wife.

Room 217—Charles Sauvé

Cramped in a corner by the window,
accompanied by Glenn Gould
playing Bach's *Goldberg Variations,*
while her father lies with tubes
up his nose, she told me
he had never said, "I love you."

When she left home to get married
she found a man who was not afraid
to wrap his words around her.

Her father, now comatose,
left her mother,
as my father had done,
for a woman
thirty years younger than she.
Mr. Sauvé's wife was now living in LA,
playing with someone her own age.

Room 217—Henri Sontag

Preceded by a large bunch of tulips
and a pair of stuffed breasts,
a leggy blond on lipstick coloured stilettos
sashayed in. Her eyes blinked
on the man lying in bed
with half his face
eaten away.

"Wrong room," she said

and backed out.

Kitchen

Another volunteer,
has set down mugs of hospice coffee.

We sit for a few minutes and talk
about our world
of potholes,
parties,
padded bras,
black panties
and the men we'd like to sleep with.

Today, the world is shaded
with the possibility of war,
lit with the possibility of peace.
Full of possibilities.

At least for us.

Room 218—Eliot Townsend

He plunged his pen in his mania
and pulled out exquisite poems.

Faced with my efforts the professor critiqued.
Sometimes he drew a funny face of approval
often he'd slash out several lines at a time.

" No clichés," he'd say.
"Keep it simple."
"Will there be anything left?" I asked.
"The poetry," he said.
"That's what's left, the poetry."

He suggested I tint this place to life.
Once I dipped the brush it began to paint itself
and, like his cancer, it took on a life of its own.

Room 218—Empty

Today, back in the professor's room
—the professor's old room—
I'm making up the bed with a nurse.

When she leaves I go to the window.
The downpour has ceased.
I look out and see nothing.

No cherry blossoms,
no geese,
no starlings,
no sparrows.

Suddenly,
a plastic bag scuds by,
full of wet light and shadows,

all we are—
wet light
and
shadow.

Room 218—Aaron Tredgett

Mr. Tredgett sits up high in his pillows,
white hair sticking out at all angles.
A bracelet of pills set before him, he smiles.

I met him a week ago, his memory clear as his voice.
He speaks my name, says the light scratches his eyes.
I lower the blind,
then sit by his bed.

He holds out his hand, I take it, gently rest it
on the heated pad by his side.

For a long second, our eyes hold.

I touched the new pink scar above his palm
that matched the scar
on his other wrist.

Room 219—Nan Umba

I respond to the flashing bell
to find dark eyes staring up
from a pitted face,
supported by a Modigliani neck.

A teenager,
beautiful, acne and all,
her baby dead, boyfriend gone
spreading his plague.

Surrounded by a zoo
of fluffy stuffed animals
in different shades of white,
she begs for painkillers.

Medication Room

Two years ago,
Nurse Verna's teenage daughter
was killed
by a drunk driver.

She enters the med. room
and unlocks the cupboard.

Even though she knows that
killing oneself is not an exact science,
she once again computes,
what would be
a deathly dose for her.

She holds the morphine,
locks the cupboard and
takes the drug to her patient.

Room 219—Myrna Underhill

Between doctor and nurse
over the patient

that fleeting glance

Corridor

An adolescent smelling of weed,
jaunts down the corridor,
hands in pockets, dark glasses,
baseball cap on backwards,
to visit his dad who's
stoned on a different drug.

An hour later
the kid slouches back,
hands in pockets, dark glasses.
He's not wearing his cap.

Room 219—Carol Upton

Mrs. Upton had been in the hospice for two weeks.
Sometimes she wore a toque.
Thursday, her head shone naked
and the family clustered in chairs around her bed.

She held up a garnet necklace for a moment
then gave it to her older daughter Sylvie,
who raised her eyebrows.

She spilled a long strand of pearls
into her younger daughter's already vaulted hands.

She flashed a large emerald ring in the sunlight
then handed it to her son's wife.
Sylvie frowned.

She slipped a small diamond ring off her wedding finger,
the underside almost as fine as a hair, held it to her lips,
then handed it to her granddaughter,
who was wearing a similar one in her navel.

Then said to no one in particular
"Possessions are the real cancer."

Room 219—Sandra Urquhart

Ian's partner, George, a surgeon,
talks to a nurse in the waiting room.

Down the corridor, in another room,
Ian sits close to his mother, listens attentively.

"It makes me sad," she says
"to think you'll never know the love of a good woman."

"Mom," he says,
"Did you ever know the love of a good woman?"

Room 220—James Vachon

Surrounded by his books, papers and a laptop,
James, a paraplegic, was dying.
It could not have been his body I was in love with,
the better part of that had been claimed by another,
more persistent than I.

On my last visit,
sitting quietly side by side on the balcony,
we watched a starling perched in a puddle,
dipping and shaking, dipping
and shaking water from its wings,

and again, without touching,
I felt his hands cupping my breasts.

Room 220—Empty

We met.

We tasted.

He died.

We wasted

nothing.

Room 220—Satish Virjee

In the late afternoon sun,
a musician fills the room
with Indian colours from her flute
for the immobile man
whose fingers that had played the piano
lay stiffly knotted on the sheet.

Room 221—Andrew Wade

While Mr. Wade lies comatose,
I bring his wife a cup of tea.
We chat.

She tells me her husband beat her.
She tells me that she'll miss him.
The sex was great.

I stand, glance at family photos on the wall
and in the reflection
see the woman
stroking her husband's stubbly face.

Doctor's Office 1

The doctor issued her diagnosis
the same way she drinks coffee—
without cream.

After leaving the patient,
I saw her in the office
writing notes
on a damp pad.

Room 222—Ann White

Yesterday,
my friend Ann was admitted.
After her oncologist left
she instructed me to go to her house,
take the shoe box
from the top shelf of her closet
and dispose of its contents.

Today,
I tiptoed for the box, it slipped,
a wad of letters fell out and
I recognized the handwriting.
Something rolled under the chair.
I burned the letters in the grate,
reached under the chair,
picked up a flamingo pink vibrator,
put it into a plastic bag
and on my way home,
dropped it gently into a garbage can.

Tonight,
I will end my affair
with that well married man.

Room 222—Diana Williams

He slowly pours warm water from a green plastic jug.
His long fingers massage Mrs. Williams' scalp.
She closes her eyes.

The thin, curly haired young man
washing her hair in bed
could have been her son.

I hold a small towel under the back of her neck.
Foam meanders along a white plastic trough,
streaming into a bucket by the side of the bed.

I unwind the cord from the hairdryer.
He, like a lover, carefully wraps and holds her head.
For a couple of seconds, I envy her.

Doctor's Office 2

Stooping over a case study,
adding notes with a slight tremor,
deep in conversation with one patient,
pacing the corridor to the next,
guiding an intern,
conferring with a nurse,
chatting to a volunteer,
knowing all our names,
always arriving early,
always leaving late
to drive home,
to catch up on new research,
to write another book
and hug
a new wife
and baby son.

Room 222—Peter Winston

The young woman lying in bed with Mr. Winston
froze as I entered the room.
I slid a red robe to the side of the bed table,
put down the breakfast tray and left.

Her hair and expression resembled
that of a model in my art class
years ago
when I and ten or so other students
surrounded her cadmium body.
With a 5B pencil, I sketched deep strokes.
Half an hour into the class, my hand locked.
Period blood wormed its way
through goose bumps down her inner thigh and
through a tiny indigo heart engraved on her ankle.

“Take a break,” said the tutor.

Pre-Raphaelite hair flowed over her face
as she lowered her head,
wrapped herself in a red robe and left.

I stopped for a moment and closed my eyes
outside Mr. Winston’s room.

Room 222—Rita Wood

A couple enter.
The patient
cringes in quick succession,
clenching her fists white.
When the mini-skirted girl
snuggles up to the woman in bed
and whispers into her ear,
she relaxes.

I leave to get them coffee and cookies
while the tattooed man in Levis,
stands, hands in pockets,
gazing through the window
at wave after wave of geese
flying in tight formation.

Chapel

Rain clotted blossoms
cascade from a vase near the altar.
This room holds memories of those
who will be remembered
eventually
only by the marks
on their gravestones.

Corridor

Your wife is here, dying.

Our distant night is black water.
After that hike a decade ago, we went back to my place.
Exhausted, we slept.
I woke in the dark, warm breath at my neck.
I turned around, slowly
moving under your warm wet hand and weight,
wishing the clearing sky, be a false dawn.

I got up and showered, felt your presence,
then your fingers kneading my scalp with apricot shampoo.
Stepping out, hair dripping, eyes smarting
I said, "It won't work, I'm married, I don't want you."

I lied.

Your daughter's been here with your wife since dawn.

Room 222—Norma Xavier

The young woman with red hair
motions me to come close
whispers in my ear
that the CIA are after her.

As her brain deconstructs
she constructs a richer life.

She asks me to take down her pictures.
I face the wall where slapdash sheets
of children's paintings hang;
I take them down.

"Take them down faster, go faster,"
she pleads. "They're coming"

Two hours later
she's dead.

Room 223—Ling Yeung

When Mrs. Yeung's family arrives
the doctors, nurses, and volunteers
stand round the bed and together
commemorate her life
in a moment of silence.

When her husband has left, we carefully
remove the hospital gown
tie a tag to her toe
cross her arms
and roll her body gently
into a large heavy-duty plastic bag.

The bag is zipped shut.
I take the last few items
of clothing from the closet and put them
into a small plastic bag
the colour of sleet hitting the window.

Conference room

In the room behind the reception desk
every other Thursday there's a meeting
to discuss the people left behind
and the help they may need.
The hour always ends
with a dirty joke. This week,
John tells the one
about the traveling salesman
and the aardvark. Though I've heard
the joke before, it's still funny.
We all leave dying of laughter.

You might see only blue sheets.
I know only the ocean
that dived into me.

Printed in the United States
63560LVS00003B/1-75

9 781424 109524